Burne-Jones
&
William Morris

In Oxford and
the Surrounding Area

Ann S. Dean, B.A., A.K.C.

MR MORRIS reading poems to MR BURNE JONES

HERITAG.

MALV.

Acknowledgements

The author is most grateful to her daughter Jackie for her help, and to the many people who have answered her questions or provided other assistance, especially: A. R. Dufty and D. Eavis of Kelmscott, Vera Magyar and Jon Whiteley of the Ashmolean Museum, Lauren Gilmour of the Museum of Oxford, Stephen Wildman of the Birmingham Museum, Linda Parry of the V & A, Jennifer Harris and Christine Wood of the Whitworth Art Gallery, Peter Cormack of the William Morris Gallery Walthamstow, Jacek Agopsowicz, Edward Evans, Donald G. Green, R. Thorp, Jim Silk, Roger Warner, the Governing Body of Christ Church for the quotation on page 19 and The Rectors or Vicars of the churches concerned.

The pictures are reproduced by kind permission of the following:

The Ashmolean Museum, Oxford, 4, 45a, 56, 58, 60, 65

Birmingham City Museum and Art Gallery, 8, 13, 31

The Bodleian Library, University of Oxford, 5 (M.S. Lat. Class. e.38. p.88.), 63 (K. P. E.1. P.1.) and the borders from the Kelmscott Log Book

The Trustees of the British Museum, title page (Burne-Jones caricature)

The Dean and Canons of Christ Church Cathedral, 17, 18, 20, 21b and front cover

The Provost and Fellows of Eton College, 50a

The Rector and Fellows of Exeter College, 48a, 50b

The Principal and Fellows of Manchester College, 32, 34

The Museum of Oxford, 33b, 46, 48b

The Oxford Union Society, 6

The Principal and Fellows of Saint Edmund Hall, 14

The Society of Antiquaries, 10, 33a, 36, 38, and back cover

Thomas Photo, 40

D. Wynne-Jones, 43

Private Collections, 21a, 45b

The Rectors or Vicars of: Bloxham, 24; Dedworth, 22; Easthampstead, 54; Eaton Hastings 29b; Lewknor, 30; Middleton Cheney, 24, 27; Tilehurst, 29

The photographs were taken by the author except for those on pages 4, 8, 31, 40, 45a, 50a, 56, 58, 60, 63 and 65 and the Kelmscott Press borders.

Other publications by Ann S. Dean

A William Morris and Burne-Jones Postcard Book ISBN 1 873089 07 4

A William Morris Christmas Book ISBN 1 873089 02 3

Medieval Life Modelmasters Collins Education

Filmstrip/Slide sets: *Medieval Background, Tudor Background, Finding out About Costume*. Published by H. Baddeley, 8 Brampton Road, St. Albans.

'There are many places in England where a young man may get as good book-learning as in Oxford; not one where he can receive the education which the loveliness of the grey city used to give us.'   William Morris 1883.

© Ann S. Dean, 1991

Typeset in 11/16-pt Plantin by Picatype, Malvern.

Printed in Great Britain by D. Brown & Sons Ltd. of Bridgend, South Wales.

Published in Great Britain by Heritage Press
1 St James's Drive, Malvern, Worcs. WR14 2 UD   Tel. 0684 561755.

A CIP record for this book is available from the British Library

ISBN 1 873089 00 7

CONTENTS

Morris's cartoon for the angel Gabriel at Selsley. This cartoon was used in 1990 to restore the damaged face in the window (see page 12).
Ashmolean Museum, Oxford

This is the first of a series of Heritage Art Guides. Each is devoted to works of art accessible to the public. The guides end with a list of the main items to be seen at each place with the access arrangements, including those for locked churches. The guides, will, however, form a useful introduction to the subject even for those unable to visit the places described. The illustrations and text include previously unpublished material. Words in italics are explained in the Glossary. Articles and books are listed under Further Reading (those which are out of print can be ordered from public libraries).

This guide introduces the work of the great Victorian designer William Morris and of the artists who worked with him, in the firm which he set up in 1861. It describes their works in forty places between Stroud and Windsor with details of access by road, and of public transport for the most important. This area is particularly rich in his firm's early windows. These have figures by Morris, Rossetti and Madox Brown as well as by Burne-Jones. Also described are unique textiles and pieces of furniture, and drawings in the Ashmolean which Burne-Jones did for Morris and for his Kelmscott Press.

Any book on Morris's art must owe a great debt to A. C. Sewter, Linda Parry, and A. R. Dufty. The author hopes that readers will be encouraged to delve into their books, see pages 68-69. This guide, however, also has new material such as Morris's bill for the Exeter College tapestry. It describes newly displayed or acquired textiles at Kelmscott and in Oxford, for example the items donated to the Museum of Oxford by Metford Warner's grandson, Roger Warner.

Detail from Morris's illuminated 'Odes of Horace' in the Bodleian, see page 71.

Morris's 1875 Ceiling at the Oxford Union Society

Many regard William Morris as Britain's finest designer. He died in 1896 but his wallpaper and textile designs are still popular. Morris met Edward Burne-Jones when they were both students at Exeter College, Oxford. They saw their first Pre-Raphaelite paintings in Oxford at the home of Thomas Combe, the Superintendent of the University Press. These pictures can still be seen in the Combe Bequest at the Ashmolean Museum. The one they most admired was *Dante drawing the head of Beatrice* by D. G. Rossetti.

In 1855 they decided to devote their lives to art. Burne Jones went to London and studied painting under Rossetti. After a year with the architect G. E. Street Morris joined him in Rossetti's studio.

In 1857 Rossetti invited them and others to join him in decorating the walls of the Oxford Union Society. The ten paintings showed scenes from the legends of King Arthur. Rossetti's scene showed Sir Launcelot (a portrait of Burne-Jones) prevented from seeing the Holy Grail. Instead he saw a vision of his guilty love for Guenevere, Arthur's Queen. The model for Guenevere was Jane Burden. Rossetti's large watercolour study for this painting is in the Ashmolean.

Burne-Jones describes how Morris ordered a mail shirt and a helmet for them to copy. One day he heard 'a strange bellowing' and saw Morris 'dancing with rage'. He was wearing the helmet and the vizor had stuck over his face!

J. W. Mackail, Burne-Jones's son-in-law, explains why the paintings soon became almost invisible - 'No ground whatever was laid over the brickwork except a coat of whitewash'. Morris finished his painting first and went on to paint the ceiling with 'grotesque creatures'. In 1875 it was repainted with the present leaves and red flowers from a 'new and lighter design' given by Morris.

Morris painted his section of the Union with *Sir Palomides' Jealousy of Sir Tristram.* Within a few months little of it could be seen except for 'Tristram's head over a row of sunflowers'. Luckily Birmingham City Art Gallery has a sketch by Morris or one of his friends of his painting, shown below. Sir Tristram is on the right embracing Iseult. Sir Palomides sits glowering on the left. The circles represent the two sexfoil windows which interrupted each painting.

Burne-Jones's painting at the Union showed *Merlin Being Imprisoned beneath a Stone by the Damsel of the Lake.* A few years later he chose the same subject for a watercolour painting now at the V & A.

Morris's 'grotesque creatures' on the ceiling are completely hidden by his 1875 design. They survive only in verse written as prose:

'Here gleams the dragon in the air; There roams along a dancing bear; Here crocodiles in scaly coats; Make love to birds with purple throats . . .'

Rossetti encouraged Morris to propose to Jane Burden. In 1859 they were married in Oxford at St Michael's, Cornmarket. In Street's office Morris had made friends with Philip Webb. He asked him to design his new home, Red House, at Bexleyheath in Kent.

Mackail wrote in 1897, 'There were no paper hangings in the house. The rooms that had not painted walls were hung with flower-embroidered cloth worked from his designs by Mrs Morris.' Two of these embroideries, *Daisy* and *Sunflower* can be seen at Kelmscott Manor. They are sewn in *laid and couched* wool on serge. *Daisy* has three different flowering plants and resembles Morris's earliest designs for tiles and wallpaper. Originally it hung in Morris's bedroom at Red House. (When the Society of Antiquaries took over Kelmscott Manor in 1962 they found it being used in the dog basket!)

For the dining room of Red House Morris planned an embroidered frieze of famous heroines. Jane described it as, 'twelve large figures with a tree between each two, flowers at the feet and a pattern all over the background.' Three figures at Castle Howard have a flowered background in chain stitch but with no trees. *St Catherine*, *Penelope* and *Isoude* are at Kelmscott, *St Catherine* (overleaf) is the only one with a tree. *Isoude* still has Morris's notes on the colours to be used. These two were repeated in stained glass.

Also at Kelmscott is a wall hanging embroidered with trees and birds. Below each bird is a scroll with Morris's motto, 'If I can'. Jane says that Morris embroidered this 'before he knew me . . . as early as 1855'. Morris felt that no one could make designs properly unless he knew the technique concerned. This is why he did this first embroidery himself but left Jane and her sister Bessie to embroider the other hangings.

St Catherine, designed by Morris for Red House,
embroidered in brick stitch by Janey (Kelmscott Manor).

Vallance says that 'a splendid wardrobe' stood in the main bedroom of Red House, 'a wedding present painted and given by Burne-Jones. Morris himself executed part of the decoration on the inner folds of the doors.' Later it stood in the drawing room of Morris's London house in Hammersmith. Now it is in the Ashmolean Museum. On it is written 'EBJ to WM'.

Burne-Jones painted scenes from Chaucer's *Prioress's Tale* on the outside of the wardrobe. He shows the Virgin Mary placing a grain of wheat under the tongue of a murdered boy so that he can still sing her praises. Later Burne-Jones painted the same subject. He also drew it for the Kelmscott Chaucer (see pages 64-65).

Jane was the model for the Virgin Mary on the wardrobe. The Ashmolean also has several portraits of her by Rossetti.

Inside the doors Morris started painting four panels. Each shows a woman in activities suitable for a bedroom, putting on her shoes, cutting her finger-nails etc. The fourth woman is only partly painted and there is a bare panel showing that six figures were planned. One woman is loosening her girdle in a similar pose to Morris's oil painting *La Belle Iseult* in the Tate Gallery. Another (detail on page 45) is brushing her hair. The letters next to her refer to the Latin refrain of Morris's poem to Jane, *Praise of my Lady*:

> My lady seems of ivory
> Forehead, straight nose, and cheeks that be
> Hollow'd a little mournfully;
> Beata mea Domina!

This poem was first published in 1858 as part of his first volume of poems, *The Defence of Guenevere*, which received bad reviews.

Vallance says that Morris and his friends were encouraged to set up their firm because the young architect G. F. Bodley promised them work. In 1861 he gave them their first order for stained glass for his new church at Selsley near Stroud.

The windows in the chancel show the life of Christ starting with Morris's *Annunciation*. Morris copied his Gabriel from a painting by Van Eyck. In 1990 the Selsley windows were restored. There was much debate as to whether the damaged face of Gabriel should be replaced from Morris's cartoon in the Ashmolean shown on page 4,

Rossetti designed the *The Visitation*. The unborn babies are shown in gold roundels on the robes of Mary and Elizabeth. *The Nativity* and *Crucifixion* are by Ford Madox Brown. *The Nativity* shows Joseph, with his carpenter's tools behind him, tasting a bowl of soup. A note on the cartoon says it was done in 1861 and was his first work for the firm. Burne-Jones designed *The Resurrection* and Morris *The Ascension* with figures taken from *Queen Mary's Psalter* which he had seen in the British Museum.

Philip Webb designed the layout of all the windows. It is partly derived from the arrangement of the late 13th century windows in Merton College Chapel, Morris's favourite building in Oxford. Thus clear glass *quarries* are used above and below the coloured panels and the yellow canopies in the *apse* are like those at Merton. Webb also designed the symbols of the four *evangelists* in the north aisle.

There are three windows in the south aisle. *The Sermon on the Mount* is by Rossetti, *St Paul Preaching at Athens* is by Morris and *Christ Blessing the Children* is by Burne-Jones. The artists used each other as models. May Morris says that Rossetti's Virgin Mary is a portrait of his sister Christina. Mary Magdalene is his mistress and

model, Fanny Cornforth, St Peter is Morris and, above him 'Judas damnatus' is the art dealer Gambart. Burne-Jones's roundel heads of St Peter and St Paul are portraits of himself and of Bodley.

Cartoons of Adam and Eve at Birmingham City Museum and Art Gallery

Under the tower is Burne-Jones's *Adam and Eve*. Following medieval tradition the serpent is given a woman's head. The beautiful rose window, at the west end, shows *The Six Days of Creation*. Philip Webb's account book shows that he designed *The Spirit on the Waters*, *The Birds and Fishes* and *Adam Naming the Beasts*. The other scenes are probably by Morris, some are adapted from Burne-Jones's rose window at Waltham Abbey (made for Powells).

Burne-Jones's cartoon for The Baptism
St Edmund Hall, Oxford

S aint Edmund Hall has the earliest Morris glass designed for a college chapel. There are six panels surrounded by Philip Webb's pattern work. In the centre is Burne-Jones's *Crucifixion*. The figures of the Virgin Mary and Saint John and the angels were designed for the college but the design for the crucified Christ was made for Amington near Birmingham.

Above the *Crucifixion* is Burne-Jones's *Worship of the Lamb*. This is a roundel of clear glass delicately coloured with *silver stain*. It shows the Lamb of God on an altar worshipped by kneeling figures. In front of the altar are the symbols of the four *evangelists*. Philip Webb's *Worship of the Lamb* in the east window at Middleton Cheney is very similar but omits the four symbols of the evangelists.

Below the *Crucifixion* is Burne-Jones's *Last Supper*. Judas is seen leaving the room on his way to betray his master. In the foreground are delicately drawn plants coloured with *silver stain*. Similar plants can be seen in Burne-Jones's *Baptism*. Below it is his *Nativity*, originally designed for Amington. It was repeated many times, usually with the same colour scheme. Another version, in a roundel, can be seen at Fawley. Behind Joseph and Mary are four angels holding candles in front of a black star-studded sky.

The other two panels are by Morris. One shows the angel seated on Christ's empty tomb with the three Maries. It was first used in 1862 for Bodley's St Michael's Church in Brighton. Above it is the scene described in Acts when two men in white suddenly appeared and asked the disciples, 'Men of Galilee, why stand you looking up into heaven?' Morris's cartoon for this panel can be seen in the Ante Chapel beside Burne-Jones's cartoon for the *Baptism*. The cartoons for the *Worship of the Lamb* and *The Last Supper* are at Birmingham.

Christ Church Cathedral has five windows by Burne-Jones all designed for the cathedral. The St Frideswide Window is the earliest. Burne-Jones designed it for the glass firm Powells in 1859. Powells had benefited from the research of the barrister Charles Winston. He had pieces of medieval glass chemically analysed to discover how it was made. Powells used this research to produce their 'new' glass. It had better colours than those previously available. Morris nearly always used Powell's glass.

It is worth comparing the bright colours of the St Frideswide Window, and the rich 14th century reds and blues in the tracery of Christ Church's Becket window, with the thin garish colours of the 1843 window at the University Church of St Mary's, designed by the architect A. W. N. Pugin and made by Wailes.

Powells made a beautiful streaky *flashed* ruby glass. Burne-Jones uses it to great effect in the *tracery* of the St Frideswide window, see *The Ship of Souls* (opposite). The actual window shows sixteen scenes from the legend of St Frideswide. Her story starts top left, with her education by St Cecilia (with an organ) and St Catherine. At the bottom of the next light St Frideswide hides in a pig sty next some sunflowers. The fourth light starts with her 'treacle' (healing) well at Binsey (see page 70) and ends with her death.

Burne-Jones' first biographer, Malcolm Bell praises 'the gorgeous mosaic of colour in the window' but criticises the 'crowding and confusion'. He says that this was caused by 'an unlucky mistake of Mr Woodward, the architect. . . . He was, at this time, extremely ill' and so 'he gave to the artist a set of measurements upon too large a scale', so the cartoons had to be reduced in size which 'affected unfavourably the clearness of the design.'

The Ship of Souls, St Frideswide Window

St Frideswide's escape

St John and Timothy, Vyner Memorial Window

The bill for the St Frideswide window is in the Christ Church archives. It cost £500 (roughly one fifth went to Burne-Jones). With the bill are letters from the architects and one, undated, from Burne-Jones. He says that he has completed the cartoons except for the *tracery* 'which I will design directly both with glass and carving.'

The cartoons for the rest of the window are in a private collection in Cheltenham. They include a few extra scenes at the bottom. Below the saint's death-bed the cartoon shows her body lying on a bier and the scene at the 'treacle' well is less crowded.

Charity, Faith and Hope (1871) are at the west end. The three figures wear coloured robes against a background of foliage.

The Vyner Memorial Window was erected in memory of a student who was killed by Greek brigands. It is one of Burne-Jones's finest windows. It contains four large figures of Samuel, David, St John and Timothy. Each stands in front of a blue *diapered* curtain (page 25). Their feet rest on a tiled floor drawn in the Renaissance way to show the perspective. The delicately shaded faces stand out against a background of foliage. *Flashed* ruby glass is used for their haloes. Their white robes are covered with a pattern of yellow leaves in *silver stain*. The tracery is filled with delicate green foliage.

Below each figure is a smaller panel showing a scene from his life: Samuel as a child with Eli, David fighting Goliath, St John at the Last Supper and the young Timothy with his mother Eunice. Next her, painted on the wall, are the letters EBJ INV (Edward Burne-Jones designed it) and CFM PIN (Charles Fairfax Murray painted it). There is only one other window signed by Burne-Jones. A drawing of the four scenes is at the Fitzwilliam. The cathedral also owns the cartoon of David and Goliath.

The Last Supper, Vyner Memorial Window

Timothy and Eunice, Vyner Memorial Window

The St Cecilia Window shows the patron saint of music playing a portable organ. She is flanked by two angels, one holding a lyre and the other a violin. *Silver stain* is used to fleck their wings with gold. Below them are three scenes from her life. Another version of these three scenes, made in 1883, is now at Cotswold Farm.

Details: St Cecilia, Cotswold Farm,   *Edith Liddell as St Catherine*

The St Catherine Window shows the saint with the face of Edith Liddell, whose death it commemorates. She was the sister of Alice Liddell, for whom Charles Dodgson wrote *Alice in Wonderland*, under the pen name of Lewis Carroll. Again angels are shown beside her (detail on front cover) and scenes from her life are shown below.

Burne-Jones's beautiful cartoons for St Catherine and the angels each side of her can be seen in the Chapter House. The angel cartoons were bought at Christies in the 1940s for five pounds each!

Morris's Resurrection at Dedworth (detail)

Rossetti's Crucifixion at Dedworth (detail)

B odley's church of All Saints, Dedworth was completed in 1866. Unfortunately it was built on clay. In 1962 it had to be demolished as the clay shrank after a dry summer and the foundations collapsed. The new church by Terry Monk has the original windows mounted in light boxes, except for Burne-Jones's 1863 *Annunciation* (now in the Centre for Victorian Art, Royal Holloway College, Egham).

The east window of Bodley's church contained three stained glass panels. These are now displayed lower down just inside the door. In the centre is Rossetti's *Crucifixion* which was designed for the church at Langton Green in Kent. It has a canopy by Webb. On the left is Burne-Jones's *Nativity* and on the right is Morris's *Resurrection*. Above them are Webb's symbols of the four *evangelists*. Both windows were designed especially for Dedworth. Burne-Jones's drawing for the *Nativity* is at Birmingham.

Morris's *Resurrection* compares favourably with Burne-Jones's treatment of the same subject a year earlier at Selsley. Webb's symbols of the *evangelists* are not shown in *silver stain* as at Selsley. Instead they are in red and blue against a green background.

There are ten more Morris & Co windows at Dedworth, repeated from earlier cartoons. They were made at different dates in the 1870s and 1880s but they have the same background of clover and hawthorn *quarries*. They are now mounted in a long vertical strip behind the altar, five on the inside and five on the outside of the church. The latter are very difficult to see except after dark. Inside, from top to bottom, are Burne-Jones's *Saints Elizabeth, Gregory, Margaret, John and George*. On the outside are Burne-Jones's *Virgin and Child*, adapted from Tilehurst, his *St Nicholas* and *St Ursula*, Morris's *St Catherine*, and Madox Brown's *St Anne*.

Morris's St Peter and Madox Brown's St Paul at Middleton Cheney

Burne-Jones's St James and Morris's St Augustine at Bloxham

S ewter describes the 1869 east window at Bloxham as 'certainly one of the most beautiful windows of the firm's first decade'. The 1865 east window at Middleton Cheney is even finer and is surrounded by other early windows by the firm.

Bloxham is a very fine medieval church. Thus it is fortunate that Morris was asked to work there in the 1860s before he made the rule, in 1877, that he would not make modern windows for 'monuments of ancient art'. In both churches the figures in the east windows are arranged in pairs. At Bloxham their feet rest on pink tiles shown in perspective. Behind them is a deep blue curtain. It has a *diaper* pattern of lions and artichokes. The same pattern is used on the blue curtain in the Vyner Memorial Window at Christ Church (see page 19) but there the lions are coloured with *silver stain*. It was also used at St Martin's Scarborough, at Peterhouse Cambridge and on a sideboard now in the Musée d'Orsay in Paris. Twelve of the figures at Bloxham are by Burne-Jones and the other four are by Morris. Particularly fine are Burne-Jones's magnificently bearded figures of *St Peter and St Paul*. Both stand in a very natural pose deeply immersed in their reading. Below them are two bishop saints, *St James* by Burne-Jones was originally designed for Southgate. *St Augustine* by Morris, has a cloak in *silver stain* (see the detail opposite). Morris also designed the bearded *King Alfred* and the two archangels, *St Michael and St Raphael*, above him.

Above the figures Philip Webb designed the battlemented walls of *The Holy City* resting on a band of blue and green clouds. At the top of the window is Burne-Jones's *God seated in Judgement* and his red *Seraphs*. The rest of the tracery is filled with Morris's angels in white against a blue cloud patterned background.

M iddleton Cheney's east window has three tiers of figures. In the top tier is a procession of figures in white and gold robes by Simeon Solomon. They are carrying Philip Webb's banners of the twelve tribes of Israel. Below them the figures are arranged in pairs in front of a hedge of different plants, oak, rose and pomegranate. Their feet rest on grass scattered with daisies and other plants. The grass is blue-green and the plants are green, a most attractive colour combination. (This was achieved by painting the plants with *silver stain* so that the yellow stain combined with the blue to produce the famous Morris green, also used for the green clouds at Bloxham.)

Adam and Noah F. M. B.	David and Isaiah S. S.	St Peter W. M. St Paul F. M. B.	St Augustine and St Catherine W. M.
Abraham and Moses S. S.	Eve and Virgin Mary W. M.	Mary Magdalene W. M. St John F. M. B.	St Agnes and St Alban W. M.

Most of the figures were designed especially for the window. They include probably the only other figures which Simeon Solomon designed for the firm: *Abraham and Moses* and *David and Isaiah*. The other figures were designed by Morris and Ford Madox Brown (see plan above). The work of the latter can often be recognised by his non idealised, individualistic faces and his interest in footwear, for example the boots of *St Paul*.

Morris's interest in surface patterns is shown in the designs in *silver stain* on the white robes of several of the figures. In places the figures overlap Philip Webb's *Leaf and Crown* border.

Middleton Cheney also has a number of other fine windows by Morris, Burne-Jones and Ford Madox Brown. In the *chancel* are panels set in glass quarries. On the south side are scenes from the life of Christ by Burne-Jones. These include the same *Last Supper* as that shown in the Vyner Memorial Window at Christ Church and a popular and much repeated *Adoration of the Magi* with a rocky background. Opposite these are two panels by Ford Madox Brown which are also seen in an 1865 window at Cheddleton. They show *Abraham and Melchisedek* and *The Sacrifice of Cain and Abel*. In small panels like these Madox Brown often treats the designs more like an oil painting than stained glass. The lead lines follow the outline of the figures. They have, however, lost their chief purpose of joining glass of different colours as most of the picture is painted on white glass.

Cain

The east window of the north aisle has Burne-Jones's *V. Mary*, flanked by Madox Brown's *St Elizabeth* and *St Anne*. Below them is heraldry by Philip Webb and above is an *Annunciation* by Morris. The next window has Burne-Jones's *Samuel* and Morris's *Elijah*.

Rather too high to see easily is Burne-Jones's 1870 west window. It shows the three *Holy Children* surrounded by twisting yellow flames in the fiery furnace. Above them are the original *Angels of Creation* and above them *Adam and Eve*.

Tilehurst has an exquisite Morris window of 1869. It has two rows of figures: five angel musicians by Morris, and a Virgin and Child by Burne-Jones. The minstrels were Morris's most popular glass design. The two playing a harp and a violin are the earliest. They first appear in some 1864 windows★. (Sewter oddly describes these windows but says the angels were designed later.) The angels with an organ and with cymbals can also be seen in this area at Lewknor and in the Ashmolean (see pages 30-31). The flaming stars at Tilehurst were repeated at Cattistock in Dorset.

The faces at Tilehurst and Lewknor are delicately shaded and are painted in *enamels*. In 1883, in a letter to Ruskin, Morris explained why he used this technique. 'Finding that it was difficult to get flesh coloured glass with tone enough for the flesh . . . we use thin washes of reddish enamel colour to stain white glass . . . N.B. this part of our practice is the only point in which we differ from medieval glass'.

It is worth comparing Morris's faces with those in the east and south windows of the chancel at Tilehurst. They were designed by G. E. Street at the very time, 1856, that Morris was briefly studying architecture in his firm. They were made by Wailes, who had been a grocer in Newcastle before he made glass.

Eaton Hastings has two very fine early windows by Burne-Jones. One shows the risen Christ, whose cloak is in 'Morris green', made by adding *silver stain* to blue glass. There is also a very fine *St Matthew*, and a later west window which repeats the archangels from Bodley's St Michael's, Brighton. All three windows have beautiful flower painted *quarries*.

★One is illustrated in Ann Dean's *William Morris Christmas Book*.

Three of Morris's Minstrel Angels at Tilehurst

Detail of Burne-Jones's St Matthew at Eaton Hastings

Morris's Minstrel Angel with a Pipe at Lewknor

Morris's Minstrel Angel with Cymbals at Lewknor

The Ashmolean Museum has two 1860s drawings by Morris of minstrels with cymbals and an organ. A grid of faint pencil lines is drawn across them to help change them into *cartoons*.

The Ashmolean's *Minstrel with Cymbals* is shown with the same foliage background on a glass panel at Wightwick Manor. The *Minstrel with an Organ* appears on blue and white Morris tiles at the V & A. These have no wings, but for churches wings were added.

Lewknor's three *Minstrel Angels* have blue robes with green patterns in *silver stain*. Opposite them are three *Adoring Angels*, two in blue and green and one in white and orange. They come from Morris's drawing at Birmingham described by Vallance and shown above. The angels stand on *Morris green* grass with blue flowers.

Detail of The Angels of Creation at Manchester College, The Third Day

Detail of St John the Evangelist at Manchester College

Detail of Hammersmith rug, 'Bullerswood' design, at Kelmscott Manor

Detail of Morris's 'Lily' carpet and border, Museum of Oxford

Burne-Jones's Miriam at Manchester College

The twelve windows of Manchester College Chapel were all made by Morris and Co in the 1890s. The figures were designed by Burne-Jones except for two by Morris. These are the Joseph and Mary Magdalene in the east window. The four *evangelists* below them were first designed for Jesus College, Cambridge. They show the influence of Michelangelo's Sistine Ceiling. Between them is St Paul at Athens with the altar 'to the unknown god'. The inscription on the altar is in Latin, *IGNOTO DEO*, not in Greek.

The most striking of the side windows are the three with *The Angels of Creation*. Each holds a globe showing one of the six days of creation. The seated angel with a zither represents the seventh day when God rested. There is no entry for these angels in Burne-Jones's account book so the cartoons were probably redrawn by Dearle from *The Angels of Creation* designed by Burne-Jones in 1870 for Middleton Cheney (see page 27). Burne-Jones also exhibited some watercolours of *The Angels of Creation* at the first exhibition of the famous Grosvenor Gallery in 1877. They are now at The Fogg Art Gallery at Harvard in the USA. Glazed terracotta tiles of the Angels can be seen at Llandaff Cathedral.

The other side windows are beautifully executed repeats of earlier designs. *Prayer* is a repeat of *St Valentine*. His blue cloak has a delicate pattern. The background of scrolled foliage with small white flowers is found in many late windows of the firm. The two side windows by the altar have a vine *quarry* background. They show Moses' sister, Miriam (opposite) and King David

Burne-Jones designed three figures especially for Manchester College. They are *Truth*, *Liberty* and *Religion* in the west window. The firm's coloured sketch of this window is at Wightwick Manor.

Morris's 17th century bed at Kelmscott Manor

Madox Brown's settee and Morris's 'Phoenix and Dragon' wall hanging at Kelmscott Manor

K elmscott Manor is a 16th-17th century Cotswold stone house in a tiny village next the Thames. Morris first rented the house in 1871. When he died in London in 1896 he was buried at Kelmscott. Janey, Jenny and May Morris lived there until their death. The villagers still remember May Morris who died in 1938. She was President of the Women's Institute. She gave talks and prizes to the schoolchildren and went shopping in Faringdon by pony and trap. May helped to erect several buildings designed by Ernest Gimson and Philip Webb in the village. Gimson's *Memorial Cottages* (1902) have a carving of Morris on the outside.

From 1871-1874 Morris shared Kelmscott Manor with Rossetti. He knew that Rossetti was in love with his wife Janey and this pained him but he felt he had no right to own her. (Rossetti had married Elizabeth Siddall in 1860 but she died of an overdose two years later.) Some of Rossetti's many drawings of Janey can be seen in the house and his first oil painting of her, *The Blue Silk Dress* (referred to in his 1868 sonnet *The Portrait*). Kelmscott also has Rossetti's drawings of Morris's daughters Jenny and May, aged ten and nine, and his painting from the door from Jenny's room.

Rossetti's studio was in the Tapestry Room. This is still hung with the 17th century tapestries which were in the house when Morris arrived. It is entered through Morris's bedroom which contains his 17th century bed (opposite). On the valance is Morris's 1891 poem *On the Bed at Kelmscott*. May Morris designed the curtains (see back cover). Janey embroidered and signed the coverlet. Her bedroom contains the 18th century bed from Walthamstow in which Morris was born. The textiles and furniture are described on pages 9, 42, 44-49 and 51, the tiles on page 39, and the wallpaper on page 43.

Tile with Burne-Jones's initials at Kelmscott Manor

I n its early years Morris's firm sold a number of painted tiles. Examples can be seen at Kelmscott Manor and at the Ashmolean. Vallance says that Morris started designing tiles early in 1862 because 'some tiles were required for use at the Red House. But at that time there simply were no hand-painted tiles in the country. . . . Plain white tiles were imported by the firm from Holland, and Morris, Faulkner and others set about experimenting with various glazes, enamels etc. . . . The same kiln that was used for firing the stained glass was made to serve for the tiles also'. They were 'exposed to the greatest heat, at the top and bottom. . . . After the first firing a soft glaze of the firm's own composition was applied.'

Burne-Jones designed several sets of tiles with fairy stories for Birket Foster and the Ashmolean has his *Sleeping Beauty* tiles of 1863. Their set does not have the border of blue and white *Swan* tiles still to be seen round the *Sleeping Beauty* tiles at the Victoria and Albert Museum. Webb's *Swan* tiles can however be seen on a fireplace at Kelmscott Manor with Morris's *Artichoke* tiles.

Burne-Jones also designed tiles with figures from Chaucer's *Legend of Good Women*. Each has a scroll with her name in Latin. As with the fairy tale tiles, two six inch (15.25 cm) tiles are used for each design. *Dido* is at the Ashmolean and Kelmscott has *Dido, Lucretia, Cleopatra* and *Philomena,* all 'martyrs' to love. The background is covered with a blue glaze which hides most of the decoration under it.

Also at Kelmscott is the only tile design with Burne-Jones's initials. It is similar to the Chaucer heroines but the scroll reads, 'If hope were not, heart should break.' Kelmscott also has some tiles by Morris showing *The Judgement of Paris*. The three goddesses are painted in a rather bright pink.

The Garden Court (detail), Faringdon Collection, Buscot Park

In 1890 the London auctioneers Agnews exhibited four large paintings by Burne-Jones, *The Legend of the Briar Rose* (*The Sleeping Beauty*). The paintings caused a sensation. One visitor to the exhibition, Robert de la Sizeraine, described 'the deep impression made on me, not only by the Briar Rose series itself, but by the attitude of the public who crowded to see it. . . . Well dressed women sitting in silence, a tiny pamphlet in their hands.' The pamphlet contained verses written by Morris to describe the pictures.

Alexander Henderson bought the paintings for his new home, Buscot Park. He insisted they should be shown free of charge at Toynbee Hall in Whitechapel so that London's East Enders could see them. Then, in 1891, he placed them in his Drawing Room. Burne-Jones designed the gilded frames with Morris's verses and did ten smaller paintings to fill the gaps between the four scenes.

Burne-Jones produced several versions of the legend. His *Sleeping Beauty* tiles, in the Ashmolean, start with the fairy cursing the baby princess at her christening feast. The paintings, however, take up the story from when the curse takes effect, causing the whole court to fall asleep. This is the part described by Tennyson in his 1842 poem *The Day Dream* but, unlike Tennyson, Burne-Jones does not show the princess's awakening. He said he wanted 'to leave all the afterwards to the invention and imagination of the people.'

First, the prince enters the rose thicket. *The Council Chamber* has the sleeping king and councillors. *The Garden Court* (detail opposite) shows three sleeping maidens round a well and three around a loom. To quote part of Morris's verse on the frame, 'No cup the sleeping waters fill / The restless shuttle lieth still.' *The Rose Bower* depicts Burne-Jones's only daughter, Margaret, as the sleeping princess.

Morris designed hand knotted and machine-made carpets. His best known hand made carpet was *Bullerswood*. The V & A has the original version. Despite its size, several others were woven and one is at Kelmscott Manor (page 33). The background colours are typical of Morris: indigo blue with madder red for the border. It measures 653 × 377 cms. Dearle's carpets at Kelmscott use purple.

The hand made carpets were called 'Hammersmith rugs' as they were produced from 1879-81 in the stables of Morris's house in Hammersmith. After that he kept the name but used larger looms at Merton Abbey. They were made by girls using Turkish knots and two inch (5 cm) lengths of wool. They followed the coloured pattern painted on squared *point paper*. Each square represented one knot.

Morris thought his machine-made carpets were 'make-shifts for cheapness' sake'. The designs were, however, so attractive that they became quite popular. The first and most popular was *Lily*. A square of this, with its matching border, is in The Museum of Oxford (page 33). It is a Wilton carpet. These were woven for Morris at the Royal Wilton factory near Salisbury. Morris & Co's leaflet for the 1883 Boston Fair says:

> Wilton carpets must be classed as the best kind of machine-woven carpets. The patterns they bear are somewhat controlled as to size and color by the capability of the machine, and they are necessarily made in strips, not more than twenty-seven inches (63.6 cms) wide, as a rule. A Wilton is therefore sewn together, and the border is also sewn on.

Kidderminster carpets, unlike Wiltons, had no pile. Morris often had these woven by Heckmondwike in Yorkshire. *Daisy*, his first Kidderminster design, is in the bedrooms at Kelmscott Manor and *Tulip and Lily* is in the attic. Heckmondwike's liked it so much that in 1878 they patented a very similar design as their own.

B elow is a piece of Morris's *Lily* wallpaper from Arlington Mill. An engraving in Vallance's 1897 *Life* and an early photograph show that this design was used in Morris's bedroom at Kelmscott Manor. *Lily* has a background of willow boughs with clumps of flowers which are similar to those in Morris's 1862 *Daisy* wallpaper.

A background of willow boughs is also found in other Morris papers like *Powdered* (1874) and they were used alone on *Willow* and *Willow Boughs* (see below) and in papers by other firms. Morris may have taken them from his copy of Gerard's *Herball*, published in 1633. Dearle's *Sweet Briar* (1912), was also used at Kelmscott. A Sandersons reprint is used at Arlington Mill.

Janey's room at Kelmscott had Morris's 1882 *Willow Boughs* paper and May's room had *Pomegranate*, one of the first three 1862 designs. The others were *Trellis* and *Daisy*.

Morris tried to print these 1862 designs himself, using etched zinc plates and transparent colours. This did not work and from 1864 until the late 1920s Jeffrey & Co of Islington printed all his papers with wood blocks and distemper colours. Later, Sandersons acquired the blocks and today they make both hand and machine printed Morris papers and also chintzes. Their *Willow Boughs*, *Willow* and *Sunflower* are used at Kelmscott today, but pieces of the original papers can be seen there.

The first textiles produced by Morris's firm were embroideries but in 1868 the firm started to sell a few printed textiles. The first were printed for them by other firms, including Clarksons and then Thomas Wardle of Leek. Morris insisted on printing the designs the old way with pearwood blocks instead of metal rollers. He also tried to get Wardle to use the old vegetable dyes instead of the new aniline chemical dyes but Wardle kept having problems. Too often customers returned badly dyed pieces to the firm's shop. In February 1881 Morris wrote to his wife, 'Tom Wardle is a heap of trouble to us . . . we shall have to take the chintzes ourselves before long and are now really looking for premises.'

In March 1881 Morris found a printing works by the River Wandle at Merton Abbey and moved there in June. By 1882 he had succeeded in reviving the difficult art of indigo *discharge* printing. Kelmscott Manor has samples of one of the first designs printed at Merton Abbey, the *Bird and Anemone* (see below). The cloth had to be 'dipped' in the indigo vat which made it blue all over. The pattern was then printed on by using bleach on the blocks.

Madder was used for red and weld for yellow. For these a mordant (fixing agent) was printed on the cloth before it was dipped and only the mordanted areas absorbed the dye. The three colours were 'superimposed on each other to give green, purple or orange'.

These dyes were expensive to use partly because, as Morris wrote in 1883, 'the cloths seem to want so much doing to them after.' They had to wash the cloth at least four times. It also had to be crofted in the sun for 3 - 8 days after the second, third and fourth washing.

Detail of Morris's paintings inside the Ashmolean's Chaucer Wardrobe

Detail of 'Strawberry Thief' chintz, patented 11th May, 1883

Kelmscott has fabric samples from Morris & Co's London show-rooms. Some still have the original price labels. They include velveteens such as Dearle's *Cherwell* and Morris's *Acanthus*. They also have a copy of the 1889 limited edition of Morris's *Roots of the Mountains*, which was bound in *Little Chintz*. Mackail quotes Morris's delight with this book and his unfulfilled intention to 'design a chintz for bookbinding. . . . calendered so as to keep the dirt off.'

Morris is famous for his wall paper designs but he preferred cloth hangings on walls. The Green Room at Kelmscott is hung with *Kennet*. This is one of the chintzes named after tributaries of the Thames. Like *Bird and Anemone* they have *branch* patterns. To Morris all patterns were based on the *branch* or the *net*. *The Strawberry Thief* uses two pairs of birds on a *net* of foliage and flowers. It has hung on the walls at Kelmscott for around a hundred years. The colours have faded but, as Morris wrote in 1889, 'These colours in fading still remain beautiful.' Page 45 shows the original colour.

The Museum of Oxford also has a piece of *Strawberry Thief*. Morris's chintzes had the firm's name and address printed on the selvage (the edge of the fabric). The address which can be seen on the detail below is 440 OXFORD STREET, showing that it was made before the firm moved to Hanover Square in October 1917. The blue selvage is typical of fabrics dyed with indigo.

The museum also has some *Tulip* curtains. This was one of the first designs which Thomas Wardle printed for Morris in 1876. More unusual are the Museum's muslin curtains. The *branch* pattern is similar to Morris's river designs but has not yet been identified.

K elmscott Manor contains a number of Philip Webb's simple Sussex Chairs, also a chair by Webb with an adjustable back and cushions. The latter was much copied in the USA where it was called 'the Morris chair' and inspired a poem by that name.

Morris & Co also sold many wing chairs. Morris started the fashion for using chintz (printed cotton) for upholstery. Most surviving chairs, however, are covered in his woven fabrics especially *Bird*. Kelmscott Manor has chairs covered in *Bird* and *Peacock and Dragon*. Stanway House has chairs in *Bird* and the Museum of Oxford has a chair in the less popular red version of *Bird*. (This and their *Lily* carpet belonged to Metford Warner, the owner of Jeffrey & Co who made Morris's wallpapers.)

The Cheltenham Art Gallery has a round table from Kelmscott Village Hall. This may be one of the few pieces of furniture designed by Morris himself. They were made by a local carpenter for the lodgings at Red Lion Square which he shared with Burne-Jones. It was for these lodgings that Philip Webb designed the Ashmoleans's wardrobe. Burne-Jones noted in his diary that he painted the outside with Chaucer's *Prioress's Tale* in 1858. On page 45 is a detail of Morris's paintings inside the doors (described on page 11). The heavy round table and the black settle at Kelmscott were designed by Philip Webb for Red House. The settle has flowers painted on fabric panels treated to look like leather.

Kelmscott Manor also has some very rare examples of furniture designed by Ford Madox Brown in green stained wood, a settee, illustrated on page 36, and beds, towel horses and washstands. As a socialist he wanted simple furniture for his own home and so he got Morris's firm to make these for his own use.

Detail from Morris's 'Bird' wall hangings in Exeter College Chapel

Detail from Morris's 'Tulip and Rose' curtains at the Museum of Oxford

Most of the upholstered furniture at Kelmscott Manor is covered in Morris's woven fabrics. The chairs in the Green Room are covered with *Bird* (1878) which he used on the Drawing Room walls of his London house.

In his 1888 essay on Textiles, Morris said of woven designs that the best plan was, 'to choose a pleasant ground colour, and to superimpose a pattern mainly composed of either a lighter shade of that colour, or a colour in no very strong contrast to the ground.' Thus *Bird* has a *net* pattern of pale blue foliage on a darker blue background. It was the firm's most popular design. It can also be seen in the Chapel of Exeter College and in red on a chair in the Museum of Oxford.

The most medieval of Morris's woven patterns was *Peacock and Dragon* (1878). There are several examples of this at Kelmscott, including the chairs in the Panelled Room and the curtains in the Tapestry Room. The 'dragons' are really *phoenixes* and the colouring and pattern are influenced by the eastern textiles and tiles which Morris studied in the South Kensington (now the Victoria and Albert) Museum.

Tulip and Rose, Morris's first design for woven textiles, was registered in January 1876. Curtains of this pattern can be seen at The Museum of Oxford and in a different colourway at Cheltenham City Art Gallery and on a chair at Arlington Mill.

Heckmondwike's wove *Tulip and Rose* but in 1877 Morris acquired his own hand operated *jacquard* loom; so Morris & Co wove *Bird* and the later designs. In 1940 Morris and Co. was liquidated and all the punched cards for the *jacquard* looms were destroyed. To make new ones costs so much that very few woven textiles are still produced.

Burne-Jones and Dearle The Eton College Adoration (page 53)

MORRIS & COMPANY.

Painted Glass,
"Arras" Tapestry,
Hand-made Carpets,
Furniture Prints,
Damasks, &c., &c.

Merton Abbey,

SURREY,

Nov: 10th. 1886

Dear Mr. Rector

We shall be quite satisfied to let the *approximate* estimate given in my letter stand as the ~~definite~~ estimate for the tapestry the sum I mentioned was 500 guineas, that is £525. This excludes the piece of panelling or decorative ~~painting~~ which I suggested for filling the space between the floor and the tops of the seats, which however would be by

small matter: but it includes all other expenses.

We have some how lost our measurements of the space, would you kindly let us have them again including the space from floor to ~~top~~ top of seats.

I am Dear Mr. Rector

Yours faithfully

William Morris

The Rev.d
The Rector, Exeter Colle.

William Morris's letter of Nov 10th 1886 to the Rector of Exeter College

Morris's first tapestry, made in 1879, can be seen at Kelmscott Manor. He called it *Cabbage and Vine*. He wove it 'with my own hands. . . . I learned the art of doing it, with no other help than what I could get from a very little eighteenth century book, one of the series of Arts and Metiers.' His notebook shows he spent 516 hours on it, using a *high warp* loom in his bedroom. Morris visited the famous Gobelins tapestry works in Paris, just as tourists can still visit them today. He was, however, scornful of the way their designs imitated paintings and said, 'A more idiotic waste of human labour and skill it is impossible to conceive'. After weaving *Cabbage and Vine* Morris taught J. H. Dearle how to weave tapestry and he then taught the other apprentices. Burne-Jones designed most of the figures. Morris, and later Dearle, designed the floral backgrounds.

The firm's most popular church tapestry was *The Adoration of the Magi* or *The Star of Bethlehem*. It was woven ten times for buyers from Russia, France, Germany and Australia as well as Britain. The first version was woven in 1887-1890 especially for the chapel of Exeter College. (The original drawing, sold by Sotheby's in 1972, showed bare hills instead of trees behind the figures.) Mackail says that Morris considered that 'nothing better of the kind had ever been done old or new.'

The tapestry shows the three Magi bringing their gifts to the stable. Joseph stands to the left clutching a bundle of firewood. The City of Birmingham asked Burne-Jones to paint a huge watercolour of the design for the City Art Gallery. This lacks the lilies and the flowers in the foreground which were designed by J. H. Dearle.

The tapestry took three weavers over two years to make. They had to wear stiff collars, even in the hottest weather, in case visitors arrived at the Merton Abbey works.

M any writers say that Morris gave *The Adoration of the Magi* to Exeter because it was his old college. His firm's bill at the college, however, shows that he charged them 500 guineas (£525). With it are his letters to the Rector (head) of the college, the Reverend J. P. Lightfoot. These show that this price was agreed in 1886 and that Morris agreed 'to submit a sketch of the tapestry'.

The bill is dated June 9th 1890 and lists the following charges:

April 20	To Arras Tapestry "Adoration of the Magi"	525	-	-
May 22	Taking tapestry to Oxford & fixing same rail & expenses	1	3	-
June 2	6 yds canvas for lining back of tapestry		7	6
9	1 pr curtains of Tulip Chintz 96700 lined and bound & also brass rod complete to hang on frame of Tapestry	8	1	9
		534	12	0

In 1890 Wilfrid Scawen Blunt ordered a repeat of *The Adoration*. His correspondence with Morris and the firm's bill are in the V & A. The letters show that Morris charged him the same as Exeter, i.e. 500 guineas, and the final bill in 1894 was for £545.

Morris's first letter to the Rector is dated September 4th 1886. In it he promises to 'make the colour both harmonious and powerful, so that it would not be overpowered by the stained glass above it. The subject suggested seems to me as good as possible for the material and the shape of the space.'

Morris's last letter to the Rector was written on November 11th 1887 and says 'We should be glad to get to work as soon as possible'. The November 11th letter shows Morris resisting the college's

request for a wider border and insisting that 'the widening of it would throw out the proportion of the picture . . . and in fact the design would have to be seriously altered'. In spite of this the 1906 version at Norwich Castle Museum does have a wider foliage border.

E ton College has another repeat of *The Adoration*. It hangs on the east wall of the College Chapel below Evie Hone's magnificent 1952 window. H. E. Luxmoore gave the tapestry to the College in 1895. He was a teacher at Eton and active with Morris in the *S.P.A.P.* in saving old buildings, including some at Eton College itself. His *Adoration* is flanked by two Morris & Co. tapestries given in 1904-5 in memory of the 129 Old Etonians killed in the Boer War. They are *Ministering Angels* and *Praising Angels* (*Angeli Ministrantes* and *Laudantes*). They are repeats of tapestries first woven in 1894. The four figures are taken from Burne-Jones's two 1878 windows at Salisbury Cathedral. (Chalk drawings are in the Fitzwilliam Museum.)

The original 1894 tapestries (one is at the V & A) have a *millefleurs* background and floral border by Dearle. For Eton in 1904 Dearle used a narrow border and redesigned the background to match *The Adoration*. Thus the *Ministering Angels* on the left stand in front of a hedge of red roses, and The *Praising Angels* stand next to white lilies, each matching the background on their side of *The Adoration*.

Below the angels Dearle added a *verdure*. This has shields on leafy branches like Burne-Jones's 1890 *verdures* for *The Holy Grail* tapestries. The three tapestries completely fill the east wall of the chapel. They live up to the claims in Morris & Co.'s catalogues that 'Tapestry is by far the most appropriate and beautiful form of decoration for a *reredos* or a blank wall space.'

Burne-Jones's Last Judgement at Easthampstead (detail)

Easthampstead has five windows by Burne-Jones. Four were specially designed for the church. The most striking is the 1874-76 *Last Judgement* in the east window. St Michael with his scales stands at the top of the centre light. Above, in the rose, is Christ surrounded by angels. Below Michael are the three recording angels and on each side of him are seated the blessed. Two pairs of huge angels blowing the last trump appear beneath the blessed. At the bottom the dead rise from their tombs. The window reflects Burne-Jones's admiration for Michelangelo and Signorelli whose *Last Judgements* he had seen in 1871, in the Sistine Chapel and at Orvieto. The shading on the white drapery bears out Ruskin's comment that Burne-Jones was 'essentially a *chiaroscurist.*'

The angels are beautifully drawn but the window lacks the brilliant transparent effect of Burne-Jones's later *Last Judgement* in Birmingham Cathedral.

The 1883 *Legend of St Maurice* on the north wall has a most unusual colour scheme. It includes a pink colour made by adding gold to the glass. Next to it is a two light window of 1878. It shows Mary Magdalene, first with the angel at the empty tomb and then seeing the risen Christ in the garden. In the *chancel* is a brightly coloured 1885 *Adoration of the Magi.*

Cranbourne has a very early window, Morris's 1862 *Christ Blessing a Child*, the design is in the Fitzwilliam. Morris's *Wedding Feast at Cana* and Ford Madox Brown's *Christ Setting a Child in the Midst* are next the font. These two panels are brightly coloured with triple canopies by Philip Webb. All three windows have pattern work by Webb.

Burne-Jones's Love and Alcestis. Amor or Love is dressed as a pilgrim
with the cockle shell of St James on his cap and his cloak.
These do not appear in the windows where Love wears a crown

Ashmolean Museum, Oxford

In 1867 Ruskin gave a lecture 'On the Present State of British Art'. He showed his audience two pictures by Burne-Jones. These are now in the Ashmolean. One is of *Love and Alcestis* and the other of the two wives of Jason, *Hypsiphile and Medea*. Both illustrate Chaucer's poem, *The Legend of Good Women*. From 1863 Burne-Jones worked on a series of designs for embroidered figures from this poem. He had already designed several tiles of Chaucer's *Good Women* (see page 39). The embroideries were intended for Ruskin, who had said he would leave England for ever and settle in Switzerland. Burne-Jones tried to distract him from this idea by suggesting that he should build a house in the Wye Valley with these embroideries to decorate it and to make 'the sweetest and costliest room in all the world.'

Ruskin's letters to Burne-Jones show that he was pleased with the designs but the embroideries were never finished. Instead, in 1864, Burne-Jones adapted the figures for stained glass for Witley, the home of the poet and artist Birket Foster and later for Peterhouse, Cambridge.

In the Ashmolean's drawings *Love and Alcestis* appear in the same form as in the windows (at Walthamstow, the V & A and Peterhouse). Birmingham has the cartoon with background drawn in. Jason's two wives, however, differ completely from the figures in the windows.

Another large drawing in the Ashmolean is *St John the Evangelist*, designed by Burne-Jones in 1895 for the Albion Congregational Church in Ashton-under-Lyne. Burne-Jones was paid £300 for the St John and nine other new figures for the north *transept* window. The evangelist holds a long scroll with the first words of his Gospel in Latin. (A Latin Bible was one of the firm's first purchases.)

Burne-Jones's Pan and Psyche.
Pan is comforting Psyche after Cupid deserted her.
Ashmolean Museum, Oxford

In September 1865 the Burne-Joneses visited Red House for the last time. Morris was planning to publish his long poem *The Earthly Paradise* with illustrations by Burne-Jones. Georgiana says that on that last visit 'the talk of the men was much about *The Earthly Paradise*, which was to be illustrated by two or three hundred woodcuts, many of them already designed and some even drawn on the block.'

Morris, Burne-Jones and Philip Webb had weekly meetings to discuss the project. Mackail says, 'Upwards of a hundred designs for pictures, including a set for the story of Cupid and Psyche, were cut by Morris himself. . . . But when two trial sheets . . . were set up at the Chiswick Press the effect was very discouraging. . . . The scheme was therefore laid aside.'

The Ashmolean has 47 of the Cupid and Psyche drawings . Others with preliminary sketches are at Birmingham, the Fitzwilliam Museum and the Pierpoint Morgan Library. A note with the Birmingham drawings explains why the Ashmolean's are on tracing paper, 'once the main composition was settled, the designs were completed by successive tracings, enabling the artist to correct his design with comparatively trifling labour . . . this was not his usual practice.'

Walter Allingham described these drawings in his diary in 1866. He wrote that Burne-Jones 'founds his style on those of *The Hyperotomachia* of which he has a fine copy.'

Burne-Jones turned many of the drawings into paintings. The drawing of *Pan and Psyche* was used for a painting for the Glasgow MP William Graham. This is now at the Fogg Art Gallery at Harvard. The painting shows Psyche naked. In the Ashmolean's drawing and in Morris's poem she wears a clinging dress.

Burne-Jones's Orpheus leading Eurydice out of Hades
Ashmolean Museum, Oxford

William Graham, the Glasgow MP, was a great friend and patron of Burne-Jones. He often slipped into his London studio to watch him at work. In 1878 Burne-Jones designed a painted piano for himself, 'to make a thing of beauty out of an ugly mass.' Graham probably saw it on one of his visits and, in 1879, he asked Burne-Jones to design a piano for his daughter Frances.

For the sides of the piano Burne-Jones chose ten roundels painted in *grisaille* with the Greek legend of Orpheus and Eurydice. These roundels are closely based on his earlier drawings in the Ashmolean. In her *Memorials of Edward Burne-Jones*, published in 1904, Burne-Jones's widow Georgie quotes from his diary for 1872 'designed the story of "Orpheus"'. Thus the 1875 date added to the drawings later must be incorrect.

In the first roundel Eurydice listens to his music, in the next she dies in his arms from a snake bite. Orpheus descends to Hades, braving the many-headed Cerberus. A rectangular drawing shows him playing his music to Pluto the King of the Underworld and his Queen Prosperine. In return Pluto allows Orpheus to lead his wife back to the land of the living, but forbids him to turn round and look at her on the way. The drawing opposite shows the fatal moment when Orpheus, alarmed by Eurydice's soundless footsteps, turns to see if she is there.

The next roundel is called *The Regained Lost*. It shows Orpheus clutching at Eurydice as she slips back into Hades. In this roundel Burne-Jones uses paler shading for the figure of Eurydice. The last roundel shows Orpheus dying of grief.

The piano itself is now in the private collection of William Graham's descendant, The Earl of Oxford and Asquith.

One of Morris's neighbours in Hammersmith was the printer Emery Walker. In 1888 Morris and Walker both gave lectures to the new Arts and Crafts Exhibition Society. Walker's lecture was on printing and Morris helped him to choose the slides. These included details from incunabula (early printed books). After this lecture Morris decided to design his own type. He studied Emery Walker's enlarged photographs of 15th century Italian types, especially those of Rubeus (see below) and Nicholas Jenson but he did not copy them 'servilely'. He wrote 'It is no longer tradition if it be servilely copied, without change, the token of life'. In January 1891 Morris's first type was ready. He hired a cottage near his London home, Kelmscott House, for what he called the Kelmscott Press.

Morris called his first type the *Golden Type* because he hoped to reprint the medieval *Golden Legend* as his first book. He had paper specially hand made by a firm in Kent from linen not cotton rags. The first sheets to arrive were too small in number and in size for the 1286 page *Golden Legend*. Morris decided therefore to print his own shorter *Story of the Glittering Plain* as his first book. It was published on May 8th 1891. The first page (opposite) has Morris's first woodblock border and a bloomer (decorated initial) designed for *The Golden Legend*. Morris had intended to print only about twenty copies of each book as presents for his friends. He feared that his pressmen would become bored if they had to print more and their standards would slip. To his annoyance, on February 21st 1891, the magazine *The Athenaeum*, described his new Kelmscott Press. The public demanded copies and so Morris decided to print two hundred copies on paper and six on *vellum*.

Aretino's 'Historia' printed by Rubeus (Jacques le Rouge) in 1476

Quefto penfiero ácora none datemere pche non puo riu cipalmente legenti tedefche mandate dalRe Máfredi(nell

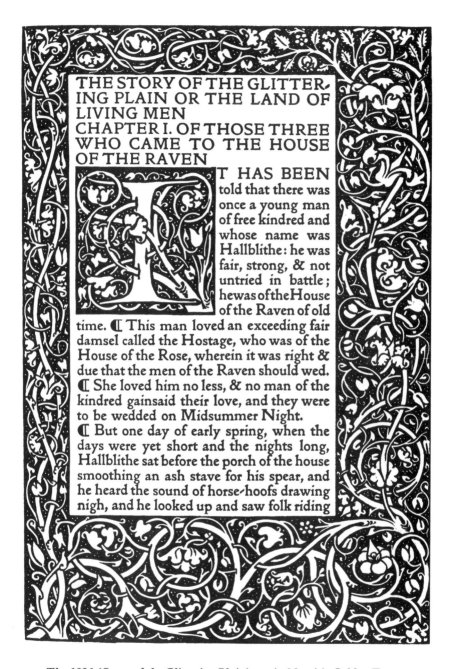

THE STORY OF THE GLITTER.
ING PLAIN OR THE LAND OF
LIVING MEN
CHAPTER I. OF THOSE THREE
WHO CAME TO THE HOUSE
OF THE RAVEN

T HAS BEEN told that there was once a young man of free kindred and whose name was Hallblithe: he was fair, strong, & not untried in battle; he was of the House of the Raven of old time. ❡ This man loved an exceeding fair damsel called the Hostage, who was of the House of the Rose, wherein it was right & due that the men of the Raven should wed. ❡ She loved him no less, & no man of the kindred gainsaid their love, and they were to be wedded on Midsummer Night.
❡ But one day of early spring, when the days were yet short and the nights long, Hallblithe sat before the porch of the house smoothing an ash stave for his spear, and he heard the sound of horse-hoofs drawing nigh, and he looked up and saw folk riding

The 1891 'Story of the Glittering Plain', set in Morris's Golden Type
Bodleian Library, University of Oxford

In 1894 Morris republished *The Glittering Plain* in his Troy type, based on German 'black letter' Gothic types. It had twenty three pictures by Walter Crane. For these Morris designed both inner and outer borders. Several of these inner borders are used in this book. They are taken from a book in the Bodleian Library in which Morris pasted the different borders and bloomers which he designed for the Kelmscott Press. A different specimen book with numbered borders is in the Emery Walker Library, at the Cheltenham Art Gallery.

Another item in this collection is Morris's hand written account of his aims in founding the Press. He wrote this on November 11 1898 for an American who was writing a paper on the Kelmscott Press. In March 1898, after Morris's death, it was printed as part of the last book printed at the Press. Cheltenham Art Gallery also has one of these printed copies. The frontispiece was printed from a woodblock cut by Morris himself from Burne-Jones's drawings of *Cupid and Psyche*.

Morris starts this note on his aims, 'I began printing books with the hope of producing some which would have a definite claim to beauty, while at the same time they should be easy to read. . . . I found I had to consider chiefly the following things: the paper, the form of the type, the relative spacing of the letters, the words, and the lines, and lastly the position of the printed matter on the page.'

His crowning achievement was the 556 page Kelmscott *Chaucer*, printed in two columns in Chaucer type (see below), a smaller 12 point version of Troy type. The first two copies were handed to Morris on June 2nd 1896, four months before he died. He designed a special binding in white stamped pigskin which was used on forty eight copies. His design for it can be seen at Kelmscott Manor.

GRECE WHYLOM WEREN brethren two,
Of whiche that oon was called Danao,

Many pages of the *Kelmscott Chaucer* have no decorations except for the bloomers. Each of Burne-Jones's eighty seven pictures is, however, surrounded by an inner and an outer border. Morris drew these with a brush dipped in a saucer of Indian ink or Chinese white.

The Ashmolean Museum has an album with about twenty of Burne-Jones's drawings for the Kelmscott Press. The drawing of Emily in the garden (above) was used for the first page of *The Knight's Tale*, the first of the *Canterbury Tales*. The final version has shorter flowers and a low wall in the foreground. The Ashmolean's unpublished drawings can be compared with Burne-Jones's drawings and sketches for the Kelmscott *Chaucer* in the Fitzwilliam Museum. These are described by Duncan Robinson in his *William Morris, Edward Burne-Jones and the Kelmscott Chaucer* (1982).

Apse   Rounded or polygonal east end of a church, e.g. at Selsley.

Branch patterns used diagonal lines, e.g. the chintzes named after tributaries of the *Thames*, such as *Wandle*. An early example is the pattern on the dress of *St Agnes* at Middleton Cheney (page 26).

Cartoon   A full size working drawing for stained glass, tapestry or other works of art. Morris & Co's later cartoons were often made from enlarged photographs of much smaller drawings. The same cartoon was often used a number of times.

Chancel   The east end of a church containing the altar.

Chiaroscuro   From Italian *chiara* (light) *oscuro* (dark); the use of light and shade to create the main effect (page 55).

Diaper   A small background pattern. In stained glass, diaper patterns were usually made by removing part of a black matt painted over the surface of the glass. At Selsley a diaper of small circles surrounds the *tracery* angels, at Bicester there is a scroll diaper and at Bloxham and in the Vyner window a lion and artichoke diaper (page 25).

Discharge   dyeing involved 'dipping' the fabric in vegetable dyes. Bleach or a mordant were printed on to make the pattern (page 46).

Enamel   In glass, a colour painted on the surface of the glass and then fired on, used by Morris for flesh colours (page 28).

Evangelists   The authors of the four Gospels which describe the life of Christ. Each is shown with his symbol: St Mark with a winged lion, St Luke with a winged bull, St John with an eagle and St Matthew with an angel; (pages 12, 23, 28-29, 32 and 35).

Flashed ruby glass. A thin layer of red glass was flashed over white glass as thicker red glass would have been opaque. Burne-Jones used streaky flashed ruby glass at Christ Church (pages 16, 17 and 19) and for the Angels of Creation (pages 32 and 35).

Grisaille   From French *gris* (grey); paintings or stained glass shaded in grey with no colour (page 61).

High warp (*haute lisse*) tapestries were woven on vertical looms. The weaver sat behind the tapestry and could only see the front in a mirror. Morris despised the low warp (*basse lisse*) horizontal looms.

Hyperotomachia   A book by Colonna printed in renaissance Italy and famed for the beauty of its illustrations (page 59).

Jacquard looms use punched cards to lift the warp threads to make the pattern (page 49).

Lancet   A tall, narrow, pointed window without tracery.

Laid and couched embroidery. The threads are 'laid' on the fabric and attached to it by small stitches (page 9).

Mille fleurs, tapestry covered with small flowering plants (page 53).

Phoenix   A mythical bird which Morris probably saw on Chinese textiles (page 49).

Net patterns are based on intersecting straight or curved lines in a lattice, e.g. *Bird* and *Strawberry Thief* (illus pages 45 and 48).

Pre-Raphaelite Brotherhood   A group of artists including Rossetti, Millais and Hunt, formed in 1848 to return art to its state before Raphael.

Quarries   Rectangular or diamond shaped panels of clear glass with a pattern in black and usually in *silver stain* as well. A background of quarries was cheaper and admitted more light (pages 28, 35).

Silver Stain   A solution containing silver nitrate painted on the back of clear glass which was then fired again to produce shades of yellow and orange. Morris also used it on blue glass to create his 'Morris green' (pages 28 and 31).

Reredos   A decorated panel on the wall behind an altar (page 53).

SPAB   Society for the Protection of Ancient Buildings founded by Morris in 1877, first suggested in a letter he drafted at Broadway Tower in Sept 1876.

Sussex chair   Rush seated Morris chair, usually of ebonised wood.

Tracery   The stonework dividing the top of a Gothic window into separate 'lights', or the glass in those lights.

Transept   The arms of the cross in a cross-shaped church.

Vellum   A fine parchment made from the skin of calves less than six weeks old, used by Morris for the covers of some Kelmscott Press books and for the pages of a few copies.

Verdure   Tapestry mainly of trees or plants (page 53).

pb = paperback, ec = exhibition catalogue.

LATHAM, David   *An Annotated Critical Bibliography of*
                                 William Morris, 1991.

VALLANCE, Aymer   *William Morris, his Art, his Writings*
                                 and his Public life, 1897 (reprint 1986).

MACKAIL, J. W.   *The Life of William Morris*, 2 vols, 1899.

MORRIS, May   *William Morris, Artist, Writer,*
                                 Socialist, 2 vols, 1936.
                                 Collected Works of William Morris, 24
                                 vols, 1910-1915 (vol 4 *Cupid and Psyche*).

HENDERSON, Philip   *William Morris*, 1967.

THOMPSON, Paul   *The Work of William Morris*, 1967,
                                 revised edition (Oxford) 1991.

WATKINSON, Ray   *William Morris as Designer*, 1967, 1990, *pb*.

BRADLEY, Ian   *William Morris and his World*, 1978.

STANSKY, Peter   *William Morris*, (Oxford), 1983, *pb*.

NAYLOR, Gillian, (ed)   *William Morris by Himself*, 1988.

HARVEY, Charles   *William Morris, Design & Enterprise*
and PRESS, Jon   *in Victorian Britain*, (Manchester) 1991.

MacCARTHY, Fiona   Forthcoming biography of Morris.

BELL, Malcolm   *Sir Edward Burne-Jones, A Record and*
                                 Review, 1892, revised 1910.

BURNE-JONES, G.   *Memorials of Edward Burne-Jones*, 1904.

FITZGERALD, Penelope   *Edward Burne-Jones, a Biography*, 1975.

CHRISTIAN, J. (introd.)   *Burne-Jones*, Arts Council Exhibition,
                                 Hayward Gallery London 1975 *pb ec*.

HARRISON, Martin   *Burne-Jones*, 1973, revised 1989, *pb* 1990
and WATERS, Bill   (good illus. e.g. The Graham Piano)

WHITELEY, Jon   *Oxford and the Pre-Raphaelites*, (Ox) 1989.

DUFTY, A. R.   *Morris Embroideries, the Prototypes pb*.*
                                 Kelmscott, an Illustrated Guide pb.*

PARRY, Linda   *William Morris Textiles*, 1983, *pb*.

*Available from Kelmscott Manor or the Society of Antiquaries, London.

FAIRCLOUGH, O. and LEARY, E.   *Textiles by William Morris and Morris & Co*, 1981, *pb. ec.*

CLARK, Fiona   *William Morris Wallpapers and Chintzes*, 1973.

SEWTER, A. C.   *The Stained Glass of William Morris and his Circle*, vol 1 Introd and illus 1974, vol 2 Gazetteer 1975.

SPARLING, H. H.   *The Kelmscott Press and William Morris*, 1924.

JOHNSON, F. (introd)   *Illustrations from the Kelmscott Chaucer*, (New York) 1973.

PETERSON, William, S.   *Bibliography of the Kelmscott Press*, (Oxford) 1984.

PETERSON, William, S.   *The Kelmscott Press, a History of William Morris's Typographical Adventure* (Oxford) 1991.

DUNLAP, J. R.   *The Book That Never Was* (New York) 1971 (Cupid and Psyche).

NEEDHAM, Paul, (ed)   *William Morris and The Art of The Book*, (New York) 1976 *ec.*

ROBINSON, D. and WILDMAN, S.   *Morris & Company in Cambridge*, (Cambridge) 1980 *ec.*

MANDER, Rosalie   Rossetti and the Oxford Murals, 1857 in *Pre-Raphaelite Papers* ed L. Parris, 1984.

CROW, G. H.   William Morris, Designer, *Studio*, 1934.

DUFTY, A. R.   Kelmscott Manor . . . *Connoisseur* 169, Dec 1968, pp 205-212.

DUNLAP, J. R.   Morris and the Book Arts before the Kelmscott Press, *Victorian Poetry* 13, 1975, pp 141-157.

LEARY, E.   The Red House Figure Embroideries, *Apollo* 113, April 1981, pp 255-258.

GOODWIN, K. C.   William Morris's 'New and Lighter Design', *Journal of the William Morris Society* 11 no 3, 1968, (Union ceiling).

There are many good value eating places in Oxford. The letters a to g show their location on the street plan on page 80.

a *The Turf*, Bath Place, is down an alley off Holywell Street, the street where Jane Burden lived. Jude's wife worked there in Thomas Hardy's novel *Jude the Obscure*.

b *The Museum of Modern Art (MOMA) Café*, 30, Pembroke Street, Tues - Sat 10-5, Sun 2-5, vegetarian specialities.

c *The Nosebag* 6, St Michael's Street (upstairs).

d *Chit Chat* 1, Boswell House, Broad Street (upstairs).

e *The Wheatsheaf*, down an alley off the High Street opposite the covered Market.

f *The King's Arms*, Holywell Street, Morris stayed here.

The Eagle and Child, Woodstock Road, interesting as the former haunt of the 'Inklings' (see the leaflet *C. S. Lewis in Oxford*).

g *St Aldate's Church Coffee Shop* opposite Christ Church.

The Perch, at Binsey, near St Frideswide's treacle well (see page 16) and *The Trout* at Wolvercote near the ruins of Godstow Abbey where 'Fair Rosamund' was buried. Burne-Jones visited it in 1854 (see Harrison and Waters *Burne-Jones*). Both pubs are on a footpath through Port Meadow by starting from Walton Well Road at the north end of Walton Street, or along the river from Abbey Road west of the station (see A-Z or OS maps or Portmeadow leaflet on sale at the Museum of Oxford). Buses go to Wolvercote; by car *The Trout* is down the Godstow Road off the A40/A43 roundabout. *The Perch* is up Binsey Lane (turn north off the A420 at the church, between A34 and station).

Outside Oxford good pub lunches can be obtained near many but not all of the places described. Some examples are: *The Clanfield Tavern* at Clanfield near Kelmscott, the *Elephant and Castle* at Bloxham, *The Fox* at Farthinghoe for Middleton Cheney, *The Waterman's Arms* at Eton, *The Black Horse* at Dedworth, *The Bell* at Selsley, *The Royal Oak* at Tilehurst and at Windsor etc.

Thatchers is a pleasant restaurant in Montpellier St, Cheltenham, behind Neptune's Fountain next a tempting book shop.

OXFORD

Ashmolean Museum, Tu-Sat 10-4, Sun 2-4. Closed a few days Sept. Chaucer Wardrobe (page 11), Burne-Jones *Danae* and the Pre-Raphaelite paintings which he and Morris admired at Combe's house.

Print Room and Basement (by previous appointment).

Burne-Jones: tiles (page 39), drawings of *Cupid and Psyche*, Chaucer's *Good Women* and *Orpheus and Eurydice* (pages 57-61), stained glass cartoons, a *Morte d'Arthur* book cover, a book of sketches for *The Wheel of Fortune* etc. and an album with drawings for the Kelmscott Press (page 65), for the Port Sunlight *Annunciation* etc.

Morris: cartoons for the Selsley *Annunciation*, (page 12) for minstrels with cymbals and organ, (pages 28 and 31) and for foliage.

D. G. Rossetti: watercolour study for the Oxford Union, portraits of Jane Morris and *Dante drawing the head of Beatrice* (page 7).

Ford Madox Brown and Philip Webb: stained glass cartoons.

Simeon Solomon: portrait of Burne-Jones.

Bodleian Library, Mon-Fri 9-5, Sat 9-12.30, guided tours, tel 277165. Morris's 'log book' of Kelmscott Press designs, all of the volumes printed by the Press (pages 62-65), manuscripts illuminated by Morris and a book binding designed by him, also medieval manuscripts which he admired; notably the *Douce Apocalypse*.

These can only be seen with a Reader's Ticket but 35mm colour slides can be inspected and purchased (unmounted) at the Bodleian Shop. Ask to see Roll 176 B (24 frames) Morris manuscripts. Rolls 345.1 (92 frames), 345.2 (41 frames) and 345.3 (4 frames) Morris's Odes of Horace (page 5). Roll 211A has Pre-Raphaelite bindings.

Christ Church Cathedral, Mon-Sat 9-5, Sun 1-5, adm fee. Burne-Jones: five important windows, (page 16-21).

Exeter College Chapel, daily 2-5.

Burne-Jones: *Adoration of the Magi* tapestry (page 51-2).

Morris: *Bird* woven textile (pages 48-49).

Manchester College Chapel, Mon-Fri 9-4. Twelve windows of the 1890s (page 35).

Merton College Chapel, Mon-Fri 2-5, Sat, Sun 10-5, 4 in winter. Webb's sketches of the windows were used at Selsley (page 12).

Museum of Oxford, St Aldates, corner of Blue Boar Street, Tues-Sat 10-5. Morris *Lily* carpet (pages 33 and 42) and *Bird* chair, *Tulip and Rose* curtains (pages 48-49) and printed textiles (pages 46-47).

Oxford Union Society, Frewin Court, Oxford OX1 3JB, tel 0865 241353. The 1857 wall paintings and Morris's 1875 ceiling design (pages 6-8). The Union has a leaflet describing these (£1.50 by post).

Rhodes House Mon-Fri 2-5. Tapestry *The Pilgrim in the Garden* (from a set of three on Chaucer's poem *Romaunt de la Rose*). Burne-Jones was working on the first of this series when he died. Dearle designed the three tapestries around 1900. For this design he used Burne-Jones's lost 1890s painting as well as his 1870s embroidery.

Saint Edmund Hall Chapel, ask porter for key, open most days. East window 1864-5 by Burne-Jones, Morris and Webb and two cartoons for the window (pages 14-15).

Littlemore, St Mary and St Nicholas (A423 3 miles SE of Oxford, locked, tel 0865 773738). Newman's Church, 1889 windows with repeats of Burne-Jones *Virgin and Child* and *St Nicholas*.

PLACES NEAR BANBURY (Oxford-Banbury X40 bus or B.R.)

Bloxham, St Mary's (on A361, 487 bus from Banbury). 1869 window with 16 figures by Burne-Jones and Morris (pages 24-5).

Middleton Cheney, All Saints (M40 exit 11, A422 500 or 508 bus, locked tel 0295 710254). 1865-1893 windows (pages 24-7).

Bicester, St Edburg's (M40 exit 9, A421). 1866 east window of south aisle, Burne-Jones: the *Three Virtues with the Three Vices at their Feet*, scrolls and tracery by Philip Webb. (The drawings for the window are at Birmingham CAG.)

Lewknor, St Margaret's (M40 exit 6, B4009, locked, tel 084 428 267) Morris 1873 *Adoring Angels*, 1876 *Minstrel Angels* (pages 30-31).

SOUTH OF OXFORD (Swindon to Lechlade bus, tel 0993 842374)

Kelmscott Manor near Lechlade, Glos, April-Sept Weds 11-1, 2-5 (apply in writing for Thurs and Fri). The house rented by Morris from 1871 onwards (page 37) with furniture (page 47) and embroideries from Red House (page 9), tiles (page 39), portraits by Rossetti, wallpaper, furniture and textiles (pages 42-49 and 51), also Burne-Jones's *Signs of the Zodiac* drawings and Morris's painting of Venus.

Buscot Park (National Trust) The Faringdon Collection (A417) April-Sept, Wed-Fri 2-6, 2nd and 4th Sats and following Sun and Easter Sat and Sun 2-6.

Burne-Jones: Briar Rose paintings (page 41).

Rossetti: Jane Morris as *Pandora*, 1869.

Ford Madox Brown: *The Entombment*, 1868 (one of several paintings of his 1865 window panel at Gatcombe in the Isle of Wight.)

Buscot, St Mary's (A417).

1892 east window Burne-Jones *Good Shepherd*, designed for Brampton in Cumbria in 1880, but with a new background by Dearle.

1897 small window to right of the altar, Burne-Jones *Angels of Paradise* (in memory of the Rector's son who died at Malvern Wells where St Peter's Church has a repeat of *The Good Shepherd* in his memory). St Mary's also has four 1920s windows including *The Three Virtues* designed for Christ Church.

Eaton Hastings, St Michael's (north of A417, near Buscot).

1874, next the pulpit, Burne-Jones *St Matthew*, designed for Marple, Cheshire in 1870.

1877, to left of altar, Burne-Jones *Risen Christ* designed for Kirkhampton in Cumbria in Dec 1870.

1913 west window, centre Madox Brown *St Michael*, flanked by Morris *Raphael* and *Gabriel*, designed in 1862 for Bodley's St Michael's, Brighton, quarries in all three windows (see page 28).

Tilehurst, near Reading, St Michael's (on A329, locked, telephone 0734 427331). 1869 window Burne-Jones *Virgin and Child* designed for the window and five minstrel angels by Morris (see page 28).

Bradfield College (near Pangbourne, tel 0734 744208). One of Burne-Jones's earliest surviving windows, designed for Powells in 1857, left *Adam and Eve after the Fall*, centre *Building the Tower of Babel*, right *Solomon and the Queen of Sheba*, striking tracery above. The cartoons are in the Victoria and Albert Museum.

Fawley, St Mary's (west of A338 to Wantage). 1868 east window Morris *St Joseph* (designed for Fawley, cartoon at Walthamstow), Burne-Jones *Virgin Mary* and *Nativity*.

Easthampstead St Michael's , near Bracknell (south of A329 on A3095, locked, tel 0344 425205/423253). Burne-Jones: 1874 *Last Judgement*, 1878 Mary Magdalene with the angel and with Christ in the garden, 1883 *Legend of St Maurice*, 1885 *Adoration of the Magi*, 1914 St Michael and two angels, (page 55).

Cranbourne, St Peter's (B3022 off A332 south of Windsor). 1862 two windows by Morris, one by Madox Brown (page 55).

Dedworth All Saints, near Windsor, (on B3024 at Wolf pub roundabout, Maidenhead buses from Peascod St, Windsor, locked, tel 0753 864591). The church has 13 windows from the old church. 1863 Burne-Jones *Nativity*, Rossetti *Crucifixion*, Morris *Resurrection*. 1873 Madox Brown *St Anne*, Morris *St Catherine*. 1877-1888 Burne-Jones *Virgin and Child* and seven saints (page 23).

Eton College, Windsor, open Easter to early Oct 2-4.30 (school holidays 10.30-4.30), tours 2.15, 3.15 (closed one day late May and late September). Burne-Jones three tapestries in the chapel (page 53).

West Woodhay, St Lawrence (5 miles SE of Hungerford). 1883 east window Burne-Jones *Crucifixion* with the cross as a tree, designed in 1877 for St Michael's, Torquay. 1887 Morris *St Augustine*, 1887 Burne-Jones *St Peter* and *St Paul*.

Farnham Royal, St Mary's (Bucks) (M40, exit 2 on A355 to Windsor, locked, tel 0753 643233 or 644293). 1868 Morris *St James* and *St Peter*, right Madox Brown *St John*.

NORTH WILTSHIRE

Bromham, St Nicholas (M4, exit 16, south on A3102). Circa 1870 east window Burne-Jones Crucifixion, prophets and saints.

Sopworth, St Mary's (M4, exit 18 A46 to Stroud and A433). 1873, next pulpit, *The Three Maries*, centre Burne-Jones, others Morris.

Rodbourne, Holy Rood (M4, exit 17, off A429 north). 1863 east window, left Madox Brown *The Fall*, right Rossetti *Annunciation*, Burne-Jones *Christ on The Cross* (Rood means cross). 1863 *chancel* west window Philip Webb *Pelican*.

Marlborough College Chapel (on A4, ask Porter, 9-1 and 2-4 term time or phone 0672 515511). 1877 repeat of Burne-Jones's *Samuel* and *Timothy* from Christ Church, Oxford but with foliage backgrounds. Morris attended the school until a student revolt in 1851. Burne-Jones's son Philip was also a pupil.

GLOUCESTERSHIRE AND SOUTH WORCESTERSHIRE

Selsley, All Saints, near King's Stanley (M5, exit 13. Walk or bus from Stroud B.R. station.) The firm's first church (pages 12-13).

Painswick, Christ Church, Gloucester St (on B4073 Gloucester to A46, bus from Stroud to Cheltenham.) 1898 east window Burne-Jones *Praising Angels* (page 53) with border by Dearle.

Arlington Mill, Bibury, March-Oct 10.30-7 or dusk, Nov-Feb weekends 10.30-dusk, these may change; tel 028574 368 or 533 to check. Morris called Bibury 'the prettiest village in England'. The Mill has some Morris items including *Wandle* and *Cray* curtains, also Henry Holiday glass cartoons and Arts and Crafts furniture, and an Albion press, like those used by Morris's Kelmscott Press.

Cheltenham Art Gallery, Clarence Road, Mon-Sat 10-5. Arts and Crafts Gallery, furniture by Morris and those he inspired, Gimson, Barnsley etc. This includes Morris's round table (see page 44) and a cabinet by George Jack who designed most of Morris & Co's later furniture, also a *Tulip and Rose* curtain. By written appointment for serious students only, the Emery Walker Library, which contains some of Morris's illuminated manuscripts and items connected with the Kelmscott Press (see pages 62-65).

Cotswold Farm, Duntisbourne Abbots. Written appointment. Three St Cecilia windows (page 21).

Broadway Tower Country Park, Worcs, April-Oct daily 10-6. Morris visited the tower. It has a Morris display with photographs.

Stanway House, Stanton, near Broadway June-Aug, Tues & Thurs 2-5. A few Morris textiles, including *Bird* on wing chairs.

Wormington, St Catherine's, near Broadway, 1912 east window, repeat of Christ Church's St Catherine with two angels (page 21).

The Thames and Chilterns Tourist Board, 8, Market Place, Abingdon OX14 3UD, tel 0273 22711 publishes an inexpensive annual book *Where to Go Thames and Chilterns*. This includes maps and lists of places to stay. They also produce free Bed and Breakfast Touring Maps: *The Heart of Britain* and *The South of England*; and *A Cottage in the Country*. The RAC and AA produce hotel guides.

Tourist Information Centres (TICs) can usually book accommodation for personal callers in their own or other areas. The Oxford TIC is at St Aldates, Oxford, OX1 1DY tel 0865 726871. It sells an inexpensive annual, *City of Oxford Accommodation List*.

Other helpful TICs with Accommodation Lists are at:

Banbury (8 Horsefair, tel 0295 59855). 487 bus to Bloxham. 500 or 508 bus to Middleton Cheney. Tel 0788 535555 for bus times.

Stroud (Subscription Rooms, Kendrick Street, tel 0453 765768).

Faringdon (The Pump House, 5 Market Place, tel 0367 242191, Easter-Oct).

Tourist Boards grade hotel facilities from L (Listed) for the simplest to 5 crown. Some hotels in each class are specially *approved*, *commended* or *highly commended*.

Some of Oxford's hotels are on busy roads and rooms facing the street can suffer from traffic noise but it is pleasant to walk through the city's historic streets on summer evenings. Here the letters A to E give a rough price guide, A are the least expensive, * indicates historic interest, in the Oxford list q marks a quiet location.

Check prices when booking, especially for single rooms.

ACCOMMODATION IN OXFORD Telephone code (0865).

Oxford Association of Hotels and Guest Houses, tel 249529

The Old Parsonage Hotel, 1 Banbury Road, OX2 6NN, tel 310210 E * (near the Ashmolean) 13th to 17th century.

Bath Place Hotel, 4 & 5 Bath Place, OX1 3SU, tel 791812 E * q *commended*.

Cotswold Lodge Hotel, 66A Banbury Road, OX2 6JP, tel 512121, 4 crown E * *commended*.

The Priory Hotel, Church Way, Iffley, OX4 4DZ, tel 749988 C-D q.

Willow Reaches Private Hotel, Wytham Street, OX1 4SU, tel 721545, 3 crown C q *commended*. Indian cooking.

Pine Castle Hotel, 290 Iffley Road, OX4 4AE, tel 241497, 2 crown A *commended*.

Greenviews, 95 Sunningwell Road, OX1 4SY, tel 249603, 2 crown A, q by lake, 1 mile from centre via St Aldates.

Pickwicks Guest House, 17 London Rd, Headington, Oxford OX3 7SP, tel 750487, 3 crown A *commended*.

Tara, 10 Holywell St, OX1 3SA, tel 244786, Listed A * q.

The Walton G H, 169 Walton Street, OX1 2HD, tel 52137 Listed A *.

(Late June to Sep: *Isis*, tel 248894 A, *Old Mitre Rooms*, tel 279821 A.)

Campsite, Oxfordshire Camping, 426 Abingdon Road, tel 24655.

Youth Hostel, Jack Straw's Lane, Oxford, OX3 0DW tel 62997.

ACCOMMODATION OUTSIDE OXFORD

The Faringdon area for Kelmscott Manor, Buscot Park etc

Faringdon Hotel, Market Place, Faringdon, SN7 8DA, tel 0367 240536, 4 crown C *.

The Bell, Market Place, Faringdon, SN7 4HP, tel 0367 240534, B*

Portwell Guest House, Market Place, Faringdon, SN7 7HU, tel 0367 240197, 3 crown C *.

Bowling Green Farm, Stanford Road, Faringdon, SN7 8EZ, tel 0367 240229, 3 crown A *, 1 mile south on A417.

Apple Tree Inn, Buscot, SN7 8DA, tel 0367 52592, 2 crown A *.

Clanfield Tavern, Clanfield, OX8 2RG, tel 036781 223, 1 crown A *.

Coxfield House, Great Coxwell, SN7 7NB, tel 0367 240568, A, see church with 'Willm Morys' brass and Tithe Barn visited by Morris.

Manor Farm, Kelmscott, GL7 3HJ, tel 0367 52620, 2 crown A-B *, 2 family rooms and 2 cottages, home of the Pre-Raphaelite author Anne Amor.

The Barley Mow, Clifton Hampden, Abingdon, OX14 3EH, tel 086730 7847, C *, described in *Three Men in a Boat*.

Ashen Copse Farm, Coleshill, Highworth, Swindon, SN6 7PU, tel 0367 240175, 2 crown A-B * small pool.

The New Inn, Market Square, Lechlade, Glos., tel 0367 52296 C*.

Banbury area for Bloxham, Middleton Cheney and Bicester

The Lodge, Main Road, Middleton Cheney, OX17 2PP, tel 0295 710355, 2 crown B *, *commended*.

Fox Inn, Shouldern, Bicester, tel 0869 345284, 1 crown A.

Swalcliffe Manor, Swalcliffe, OX15 5EH, tel 029578 348 March-Nov only, 3 crown B *, next to medieval church and tithe barn.

Thatched House Hotel, Manor Rd, Sulgrave, OX17 2SE, 3 crown C *, tel 029576 232, opposite Lawrence Washington's Sulgrave Manor.

Easington House Hotel, 50 Oxford Road, Banbury OX16 9AN, tel 0295 259395, RAC B-C*, home of daughter of Lawrence Washington.

Tredis G H, 15 Broughton Road, Banbury, tel 0295 4632, 2 crown A.

Near Reading and Windsor for Easthampstead, Eton etc

Manor Farm, Brimpton near Reading, RG7 4SQ, tel 0734 713166, Listed A *, 18th century with Norman chapel in garden.

Sir Christopher Wren's House Hotel, Thames St, Windsor, SL4 1PX, tel 0753 861354, 4 crown E *

Youth Hostel, Edgworth House, Mill Lane, Windsor SLA 5JE, tel 0753 861716 *., in Clewer, 1 mile from Windsor off A308, via A332.

Woodlands Park Farm, Ashford Hill, Newbury, RG15 9AY, tel 063523, 2 crown A *, golf, riding.

Near Stroud for Selsley and Cheltenham

The Grey Cottage, Leonard Stanley, Stonehouse, GL10 3LU, tel 0453822515, 3 crown B * *commended*.

Down Court, Slad, Stroud, GL6 7QE, tel 0452 812427, Listed A * *commended*, 17th century, filmed in *Cider with Rosie*.

Royal Gloucestershire Hussars, Frocester, tel 0453 822302 A*

Elmtree Farm, Frocester, Stonehouse, tel 0453 823274, 2 crown A *, *commended*, April-Oct only.

Old Vicarage, 167 Slad Road, Stroud, tel 0453 752315, 3 crown A-B

Calcott Manor, Beverstone, Tetbury, GL8 8YJ, tel 0666 890391, 4 crown E * *commended*, heated pool, Michelin starred restaurant.

Bowden Hall Hotel, Upton St Leonards GL4 8ED, tel 0452 614121 D. Cotswold Farm's St Cecilia windows (pp 21 and 75) came from here.

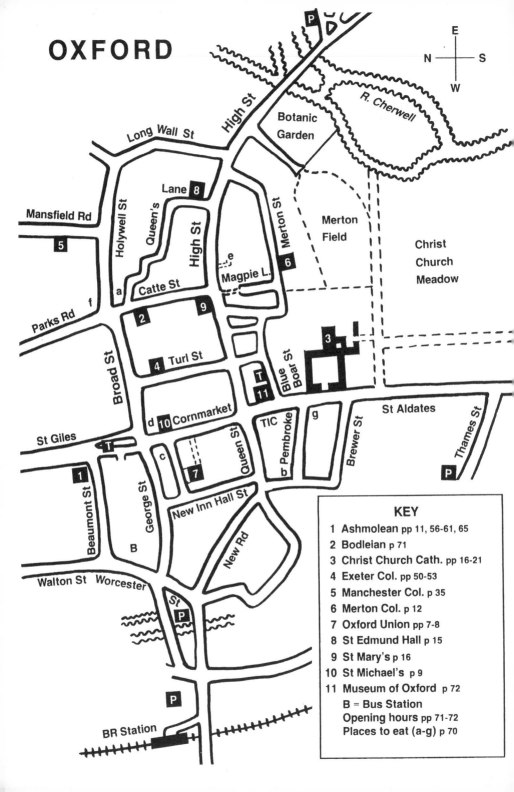

OXFORD

Long Wall St

High St

Botanic Garden

R. Cherwell

E
N · S
W

Mansfield Rd

Holywell St

Queen's Lane

8

High St

Merton St

Merton Field

Christ Church Meadow

5

e

6

Magpie L.

a

Catte St

f

Parks Rd

2

9

4 **Turl St**

3

Blue Boar St

Broad St

T
11

St Aldates

d **10** **Cornmarket**

TIC

g

Brewer St

Thames St

St Giles

T

c

Queen St

b **Pembroke**

P

1

Beaumont St

George St

7

New Inn Hall St

B

New Rd

Walton St **Worcester**

St

P

P

BR Station

KEY

1 **Ashmolean** pp 11, 56-61, 65
2 **Bodleian** p 71
3 **Christ Church Cath.** pp 16-21
4 **Exeter Col.** pp 50-53
5 **Manchester Col.** p 35
6 **Merton Col.** p 12
7 **Oxford Union** pp 7-8
8 **St Edmund Hall** p 15
9 **St Mary's** p 16
10 **St Michael's** p 9
11 **Museum of Oxford** p 72
B = Bus Station
Opening hours pp 71-72
Places to eat (a-g) p 70